Pr River Valley

"The superpo isly he repeatedly and the environments he builds. His relationship with place able, breathing entity and his desire for you to get there, too. *Green River Valley* is a book that continues in this lineage. You are present in the poems, with the buildings, with the neighbors and mothers and the songs of birds. So much gratitude for this offering."

— Hanif Abdurraqib, author of *The Crown Ain't Worth Much, They Can't Kill Us Until They Kill Us, Go Ahead in the Rain*, and *A Fortune for Your Disaster*

"Robert Lashley has achieved the impossible. *Green River Valley* brings the epic scope of history into an intimate kiss with language and the body. After reading this book, you will never be the same, you will see life, love, pain, joy, beliefs, the world, everything you thought you knew, differently. This book is a new kind of existence, one where the hugeness of history and the whisper of one person sighing into the night are not distanced, where the voice of God and the voice of the street or the bar or the bus are not separated by a strange and wrong story of heaven separated from earth. Make no mistake, this is holy ground. Take a drink. Dance until you drop. Cry a river. Let desire do what desire does, unbound. This book sings a body back to life. This book is blackness in motion, giving the cosmos and the rest of us a chance to get the story back. And aren't we lucky to have someone capable of this depth of brilliance threading through language, love and voice? This book will deliver you."

— Lydia Yuknavitch, author of *Verge* and *The Chronology of Water*

"Robert Lashley is my 'Brother Mystic,' for real. This book is at once a battle, a surrender, and a journey. It is a powerful musing on place and its deep impact on how we experience humanity – both in spite of and because of who we are. Lashley does not shy away from the complexities of Blackness. More specifically, how to be Black and male is to be party to a legacy of exquisite beauty, as well as an historical devotion to misunderstanding and dehumanization. But Lashley knows better and shows the reader, too – through unique, haunting and sometimes disturbingly witty pieces. His work seduces, warns, teaches, and call us forth to receive the blessings of all the places we call home – family, nature, spirit, self – no matter how much they've scarred us."

— Kellie Richardson, Tacoma Poet Laureate (2017-2019)
and author of *What Us Is* and *The Art of Naming My Pain*

"Robert Lashley is part literature scholar, part street preacher. He has long reached equally into the depths of history and culture and into the smoky dives and shadowy street corners of 'Grit City'—Tacoma, Washington—as fuel for his achingly beautiful poetry. And in *Green River Valley*, his powers—his rich mind and his wounded soul—blaze in glory like never before."

— Samuel Snoek-Brown, author of *There Is No Other Way to Worship Them*

"Elegantly sung and astutely political, Robert Lashley's poems detail the pleasure and violence of everyday life in *Green River Valley*, on the streets of Tacoma and Seattle, over Salish shores and waterways, among birds in smoke-filled trees. Intellectually ferocious, Lashley's work situates his vision among both canonical poetic history and contemporary public life. Gentrification and capitalist excess clash with hope and beauty on sidewalks where 'Winter birds and buzzards

... make their wobbly transits. / The last standing deacon could not find his wings / so he lowered his hands in the snow.' This brilliant book is vital to contemporary literature, a poetic history of a rapidly changing place, a celebration of Black lives lived, and a tour de force critique of the exclusionary literary canon that seeks to marginalize art crafted outside white privilege and the Ivory Tower. The voices in this book tell stories of survival and pain, but also longing and optimism rooted in music and creative engagement. In 'Value Village,' Lashley sings of love: 'My dear around-the-way girl, / dance with me by sale colors. / Time may erase all style to memory / but the intercom is playing our song.'"

— Carol Guess, author of *Girl Zoo*
and *Doll Studies: Forensics*

"Robert Lashley's poems go beyond the human to find the being. Like Gergely Dudas' puzzle paintings, he focuses attention on the ordinary until the extraordinary emerges from its midst. There is, in this collection, a longing, a manifesting of the disquiet. Poems as x-rays. Lashley sees the psychological crocodile mingling with underwater vegetation and moves aside the reeds and bulrushes for a judgment-free, clearer view. His intellectual breadth and depth are breathtaking; his intimacy with life-stripped-bare, illuminating."

— Lola E. Peters, editor-at-large for the
South Seattle Emerald and author of *The Truth About White People* and *Taboos*

"A nation, a myth, a beat, and a revolution walk into a bar. What happens next is extraordinary. Seriously, *Green River Valley* is a confrontation of powers and the result is a poet on real terms with what it means to love in times of violence and loss, what it means to write in times of silence. These poems aren't read so much as thumped into the chest, and its truths are unhidden, unmasked. When Lashley writes, "To see is too much. / To not see is much more" I feel like the past and future of any city, but especially Tacoma, make sense."

— Abby E. Murray, Tacoma Poet Laureate (2019-2021) and author of *Hail and Farewell*

"Lashley's writing transports readers to places and moments that teach us, remind us, and challenge us. His stories have a distinct texture and evoke grief, joy, and the unnamed places in between. *Green River Valley* is a journey that engages all of our senses from the soul to the bone."

— Thy Nguyên, co-organizer of The People's Assembly and former Tacoma Poet Laureate (2015 - 2017)

Poems by

Robert Lashley

Green River Valley

Cover photography:
"August 19, 2018 • Tacoma, Washington" by Jody Poorwill

Cover design & layout by Knic Pfost

Editing by Christina Butcher & Kate Threat

ISBN: 9781733037587

Blue Cactus Press | Tacoma, Washington
bluecatuspress.com

Poems by

Robert Lashley

To my people here:

Uncle Gee, Chris, Fab 5, Team Mayo, Anna, Gary, Michelle, Sarah, Graham, Conn, Skyler, and Jessica:

Thank you for being there as much as you could during a rough fucking time. I honor our friendships and how they have made a better person.

To the people who took a chance on me:

Matty and Carrie:
Thank you for publishing my first two books. I had some of my best memories of my life with Small Doggies Press, and I will always hold you in the highest regard.

Christina and Everyone on team Blue Cactus:
Thank you for bringing me back from the wilderness.

To my people gone:

Uncle Mike, Uncle Robert, Aunt Essie, Aunt Willa, Aunt Eulalah, Aunt Virginia, Aunt Pat, Aunt Marilyn, Jermaine, Lisa, Momma Salty, and Momma:

I love you in a place that has no space or time.

This book is dedicated to my Momma. You once read me poems to beat back the blues of the foodbank line. I will read poems for you until the day I see you again.

Contents

The Revolution Will Not Be Cat-Called, And Other Notes on The Niggas That Came on The Bus from Shahrazad's

Parts of this poem are influenced by T.S Eliot's "Ash Wednesday"

1.

"'Black men, she says, are shouting praises about her controversial appraisal of black women. The entire community will get a chance to hear that appraisal tonight when Ali speaks at the Paramount Theatre at 8 o'clock. 'Her truth is so to the point that a lot of black women don't see how they can effectively address some of the issues,' said Curt Smith of Seattle.'"

– "Shahrazad Ali Points Finger at Black Women —
Controversial Author to Speak at Paramount Theatre
Tonight," *Seattle Times*, October 3rd, 1990

Nation time is always on a workday.
The fantasies of prodigals crowd
bus stop assignments; the comings
of judgment over penciled inventories,
with shrapnel and flank used by ankhs
in wars that they mistook as revolutions.

Revolutionaries start where no drivers see.
The infirmed glory of the five percent hour
is a Byzantium for the dumb and blind.
Holy gestures strut and proclaim the vein
of the third eyes' transitory power.
Men smush their heads in oil and ash
as the bus goes by green water.
Nouns and verbs, they twist your face
as the bus goes by the green water.

And pray to the driver to have mercy on us.
And pray for the stops when men may forget
the altars where the saved may see us,
the fire of the valley of the double seat,

the parabolist's floor in the minutes and hours
where the men start to look for calves,
where those who are dead can't come alive again
and those alive see nothing but harlots.

Pray! Pray, homeboy! Pray for the quiet!
Matters much discussed and little explained
are sermons for prayers too answered,
are judgment hands laid too heavy upon us.
Pray!   Pray for calm.

2.

"Don't you move your goddamn ass to Seattle, Glennis. Niggas filled up the paramount to hear somebody say I should get my ass kicked. Niggas filled up the paramount to hear somebody say I should get my ass kicked. Niggas filled up the goddamn paramount to hear somebody say I should get my ass kicked."

– Big Momma, October 4th, 1990

Buses stop where no gates swing,
where no stars burn or trumpets sound,
where no plagues or woes cause
agony but to those without two bucks.

Three OG's and thirty-three elders sat under
the poster of Pierce evergreens.
Inside cool rain, the northern signifiers
(king boys transfixed by the paramount word)
fixate on hips, lips, and licks,
fixate on their grinders of humans into dreams
their negatives a piecemeal of the blues
their negative in endless city phantasms
of gods and demons, immobile and fluid.

Shall our bones live? Shall our bones live?

And that which had been contained by the stop changes
start to speak and speak and speak.
The ankh boys make their altar calls
In binary two steps with love and death.

My muse! My mystery lady!
My goddess creature!
Come drink me of your loveliness.
Be my virgin and labor for me and serve as Queen
of my bus.

Bus mirrors are filled with convex angels
in their descents to Hades' dream kingdom.
C'mon baby
What's wrong, bitch
Goddesses are defrocked in Athena's backs seats.
Bitch
Ho
Cunt Dyke
Bitch Ho
Bitch

The posterity of the singles bar
and the nation's guided wants.
Let a madness of bones free near the home stop.
Bitch
Bitch
Bitch bitch bitch bitch bitch bitch

Oh, my niggas what have we done to thee?
We
who walk between the violent and the violets,
who walk between the various ranks
of gilded cages,
strangling veils, and rings inversed
in the colonnades of golden pedestals.
Singing of survival things
among the ignorance and knowledge of man's eternal dolor
Who moves among the brothers as they crept?
Who makes strong the shut-in, hiding, elusive?
Make strong the door and the lock key.
Make strong our new verses of ancient freedoms,
our unseen vision in your future dreams
while jeweled macho men signify our hearses.

Neighbor sisters who spread sage in black and blue
sigh and speak no words.
Garden mothers in the creases of shadows

sigh and speak no words.
Flaked gods flail as ghetto birds sing down
in the land of our sectioned exile.

Oh, my niggas what have we done to thee?

Will your Black god pray for those who offended them?
Those terrified of his mirror but who cannot surrender
on the cliffs above his black rock.

Oh, my niggas, what have we done to thee?

If the Black world is lost, if our love world ain't love,
If the unheard, unshaken black word is freedom,
where is the world you knead off our skulls?
Where will your Black god minister to those
who walk in his darkness,
who are torn between season and the season of bills,
time and time of the rent man,
the hour and the hour of little niggas at the kitchen,
who will not go away yet cannot pray to you,
for your miracles have hollowed their eyes?

The Next Day

Although I cannot hope to rest again.
            Although I cannot hope.
Although I cannot hope rest from
wavering between street prophets,
lost boys tweaking in the corner store.
In the moving traps of a hundred hero's journeys,
in schizoid twilight between father and motherlands,
            I do not wish to wish this shit.

Ferries – visible and non – cross on Salish shore.
Third eye windows dance with suburb doors.
Men speak of corralling and leading in the smoke
while the witches must work this morning.

The beige fog stiffens among the noises.
The lilacs are masked, and the church bells echo
and the tired spirit quickens to a rest
            on the 27 bus.
It quickens to forget the blood fight
            and the prodded symbol,
the Hotep forms and the ivory gates
in a window space to rest on this bitter earth.

The ghetto nerd's tension
is between dying and re-birth,
the distance from solitude where all tribes cross
between the murked and the green meridian
where voices shaken from wild mouths
            drift away.

To suffer one's self is to mock nationhood.
To care and to not care as people run to their rocks.
To suffer one's self is to be separated
by the dividing lines from the corner to the sea.

Storefront Preacher Man's Last Testament, 11th & Commerce

What is a camel to a needle in the defrocked eye?
What is a needle to a bottle in artisanal streets
that adapt hard to the resignations of winter?
Its binaries of color mask and accompany
but defy invisible ice pews.

At his sermon on the frost, the wandering tribes
lose their patience.
Kindreds who cannot wait
for frozen altars
move past his reheated texts of Sodom,
move past the stretching of his blue-black hand
for something to carry him,
for a ladder to roll with the fallen sky,
for a golden stair to bless his sacrifice
of a dream-colored boy and his nature.

Unions and successions dissipate in his death story
yet salt does not freeze, stones do not raise up.
Blades he called the rolling arch of his sacrifice
reappear as metaphors in his tongues,
reappear as the countenance of his dead lambs
on city buses
that vanish when their black smoke is gone,
that vanish with the harbor sounds light break
as city lights stop their constellations,
as last turtledoves below old new lamps
make their wobbly transits.
Winter birds and buzzards, infirmed and aged,
make their wobbly transits.
The last standing deacon could not find his wings
so he lowered his hands in the snow.

Hillside Terrace Memorial Commencement Poem

The Double Dutch crew runs in the late day.
They kick it and take-off briskly.
They elude the potholes of the changing same block
rebuilt as an amazon trap.
In the morning, when we rise.

They fly past upturned and upturned lands.
They fly as the soil is flexed from the hill
where the adults left are men,
the men left are boys
and the children were already dead
before new buildings got sided.
In the morning, when we rise.

They fly past the block's starless air.
They fly as the men set trip and fall
below shadows of stone crosses.
Below the road is a mirage of the riverbanks
with gilded stars and ill-cast buckets,
ritual stones that pave all progeny.

They fly and become the redlined gourd,
an end and beginning in aspirant ground
where children are parents to trap gods,
where cops push hoods to the side of the road
for the path of gangster soccer dads,
where emcees pose then pop their white collars
then make mixes from bones to Milly rock to
where reenactors troll and patrol
then Crip waltz for imagined lands.
In the morning, when we rise.

They rise over the set trip meridian
riding over skyscrapers and shelters false and gone
circling trains, treaties, and generations
of blood calls.

As I Turn Down His Offer to Buy a Television for Five Dollars, America ...

Laughs as he does his twitch dance
laughs as he slaps the ash of his hands
on your palms, then pops his collar
tells you his suit is dirty because
he was painting the town so red
and the night was so crazy
and out of control
that he lost his other shoe;

and if you let him hold something
he'll take care of his kids this time
and if you let him hold something
he'll make it right with the folks
he fucked over
on the blocks down the street
and if you let him hold something
he won't let her take the rap anymore
and will never call her a bitch again
and if you let him hold something
he'll get you back
and y'all be rocking them chains
like he used to.

Two Old Hill Survivors, When the Thrown Fireworks Get Too Close to The Wall

My body is a rumbling evening train
take it and find what is feeling for you.
The room that you take never takes space
take what you need from my arm.
Look, the lovers have stole away.
Look, the lovers are gone.

The bomb is the abyss beyond reenactments.
The bomb is the maker of time, tempo and pitch
and summer soldiers acquire a winter in their bones.
Look, the lovers have stole away.

And sobriety is a struggle for reliable forms
in the spaces between trauma and traumas.
In the apex of the sunshine patriot, please take my palm.
Look, the lovers are gone.

Seek yourself first in the frames of my chest.
Seek out the infinites under the contours of our walls.
Look, the lovers have stole away.

Seek through their buck shots your own hiding place.
Seek in my broken columns your own city of refuge
under the firecracker's misguiding star.
Under the Antichrist's ultramarine by fire
I need not believe in what is actual.
I need not verify to believe i n that portal
your love is both real and a dream.
Your love is my evidence of all that's unseen.
Look, the lovers have stole away.
Look, the lovers are gone.

Missing LL, Walking from People's Park to Althemier Church, 5:30 AM

Light breaks in opposition to the heart.
In unduly lights, in shocking stints
in uneasy shadows of neon fronts
that bloom to homie ghosts.
Children who were parents to hoods
and homies who had their time drawn here.
The heaven and hell of the actual
is in the proximity of the gas can,
is in the proximity of the strewn visions
of street shepherd and lamb's
and piper men's strolls from humanity.

In the mourning park, from wrung out eyes
boombox sambas reverberate walls.
Spins paint light from black-blue dawns,
refracted day-to-day from the unseen.
Refracted needles and lines are rings
as I turn in the burnt blue to see us:
the hoodlum and the goth nerd mama,
the bullet gown and the brown, ragged suit
hissing at those who hissed,
creating spun sundials over black hats
in a two-step kingdom from memory.

Resurrections illuminate repainted walls.
Niggas and nightmare dream of nymphs
are refurbished by the tagger's eye
          and the ragamuffin emcee
spitting in tandem with the stale gospeller.
In the morning, sight is a turned-young dream
          of love engulfed by flames.
L- dawg
          Sis money,
                              OG lily of the valley.

My song could not raise you from these flames.
My ladder could not bring you above the door
And my back broke in 90-proof hives.
My song could not bring you or us from hell.
I sing just to know I am alive now.

Song of the Triple OG Bird Rescue Man

Blood is the color that mixes late September.
It tints the concrete of a late sunset mass.
It makes a mass of niggas and blackbirds.

The OG in white will take them.

It is on wings of those beat and broke in migrations,
those caught up in wounds and rickety structure
those lost in aroma's poisons and intoxicants
allusive until they couldn't breathe.

The OG in white will bring them.

Allusive is the errant gangsta disciple
as he washes his pavement of red.
Allusive is his second act with body bags
and his church with invisible chimes,
and his yellow tapes fluttering in the leaves
and dust-to-dust coloring everything around it.

Lord, I'll go sweeping through the city
where my hood niggas have rolled before.

The old man claps, and cleaner particles
become a set of flying night birds.
The old man claps and ruins of a playground
become neither ruins nor a playground.
The arcs of the busted jungle gym
lift and re-sheath their pipe swords,
lift every rock that interacts with his ash
as the swing set chains stop their hanging.

The OG in white will bring them home.

At dusk, home goings are everywhere.
Agony moves through Anglican storefronts.
Agony lies still in the gravel.
Dope boys barely make their stops now.
Dope fiends run to the water.
At dusk, the OG finds place after place
to give rosaries and proper burials.

I will stand someday by – by the river.
Won't be back on this block no damn more ...
The OG in white will take them.
The OG in white will bring them home.

Soft Boy Barbershop Death Fugue

A boy's first death is when men rob him of color:
the first snap from creation – in a chair – in a line.
The men remake him and make him dream of the river.

Purple highlights are snapped in order. He trembles.
The abyss becomes a buzz cut, then a smack to his spine.
A boy's first death is when men rob him of color.

The men surround him–prod him–flash out their temper
then thrust their masks upon him in turns and in time.
The men remake him and make him dream of the river.

They prod and they chant, "Am I my brother's keeper?"
Yet the kept cattle boy's is piecemeal and twine.
A boy's first death is when men rob him of color.

And then the kings are happy–finished–over.
And the blank-slated boy their drum circle shrine.
The men have remade him and made him dream of the river.

In the potter's house, the one God eats the sparrow.
In the potter's house, Sabbath is blood on the vine.
A boy's first death is when men rob him of color.
The men have remade him and made him dream of the river.

If, My Niggas

For the young creatives kicked out of the Tacoma Public Library by the police for lingering, in which I re-run the jewels on Rudyard Kipling

If you keep your head on a life of swivels
in the walking shadow of perpetual fades,
if you lose trust when all doubt your witness
and make allowance for guns – and gats – and blades,
if you can't wait, and can't be tired of waiting
or being lied about, but cannot survive the lie,
or being hated, and cannot afford the hating
because you look too "you" and talk too wise

If in their dreams, they dream of masters,
if they think and make your thought their aim,
if feet are the measure of triumph and disaster
and your life can't afford them just the same.
If you can't bear to hear the truth you've spoken
twisted by mall cops and traps and fools
or watch the things you made, broke and rebroken
then sold as not your own, with worn-out tools.

If you can run from the game when its winnings
are risked on your bodies' pitch and toss,
with corpses swept at each beginning
and never a breath about or a word about loss,
if you can never betray your heart and sinew
and honor your kinfolk long after they're gone
and hold when the players take everything from you
then cry and say to themselves "hold on."

If, in the caverns of learning, there is no virtue
and in the trap cave there is no common touch,
if young ones in revolving tombs can hurt you
with men who count nothing and then count too much,

if dead body dream fills the unforgiving minute
no matter then distance or space, loved ones, fly.
Our triggers in the city are a river of sight
but to stay and ponder them is to die.

On the Day That Last Black Body Is Shot

There will be burning lavender

and concentric crowns of sage
that spin
above alleys, woodsides, and corners.

And embers that rest around the shadow men
that swing from dead gates
to play tambourine.

Their high notes will be the sign
that figures everything around them,
that rebreaks and washes clean
every chain and every courtyard
that melts every 44-revelation trumpet
to a moving river of altars.

And the concrete will churn
those who can't raise.
And every hood of a deli
and deluxe squad car
will be replaced by windows with our faces
and scavengers of our bodies and kneecaps
will go blind
where the shadow men affix their breakbeats.

And the world will be lit
by a neon upper room
with the rosebush thrones
and colonnades of sage

And lilies will sweep the dead
from 10,000 valleys,
lit from the lights flashed

on our bodies
charged from the codes
they turned to curses.

They will rest on clouds of joy.
They will rest on clouds.
They will rest on.
They will rest.
They will.

Steampunk Junkyard Artist Sonata

I flip some Ezekiel

A Teamster signs swings
above arboretum glass
on a copper nail.

With the wind, project sidings
link nation meeting rooms
and rib shacks.

Trap houses and chop shops
come together in their holes.
Car doors and sinks
through propped windowpanes
are moving constellations
on the gravel.

Around the limbo of renewal
the wind is a mentor.
To define here is to be vast,
to be finite in heft,
to be a god, arbitrary
yet lonely
yet common under shiny new mass.

In gusts, nature demands
to eliminate canons,
to see new variations
as the wheel within the wheel
the mother of metaphor
the black tarnish stone
where dry bones
get up walking all natural
the direction forward
when all directions are gone.
The turn without a gaze
at what's leveled.

The Proud Boy Cop at Freight House Square

What a blind god promised, his Caesar delivered
in codes, torches, and guttings that skew
toward oblivion's convex mirrors.
His Christ is a two-headed hydra that spews
Blood the deluded mistake for angel dust,
his ropes mistakenly fit as robes
in Puritan troll city sweeps,
his solution for gentrified soils
his dream of Eden, with a paved-over past
and a North Star's too distant sliver.

The hill is not the ladder of divine ascent,
it is the precinct where this bike cop roams
ladders and potholes are impostors
in the designed shadows of renewal.
The blue guard imagines only he can imagine
the means and ways to your end.

But where are his black heralds?
Your body that he calls on won't hide him.
Your blood that he calls, as folks run to their rocks
blurs not slave and free, but his rosy cheeks.
His set trips bend but can never break
our shared bones, bonds, and interred uniforms
that a blind god deemed expendable
and his Caesar made perversely new.

You and I, blood, are both down by that river.
I'll go, yes, but then they'll get you.

Landscape with the Lightning That Told Me to Stop Writing Poems in Wright Park

Branches that flash
the lightning of their veins.

A globe atop a leaf moat.
A leaf moat atop a globe
of re-dead matter.

A phylum within the dark
that poses, highlights,
then goes back to the underworld
of recycled blackness
at the receded memory of a flash.

To see is too much.
To not see is much more.
To connect – to find and alchemize a moment –
is the solace of the pen, flash, and eye.

Elder's Last Sea Shanty

For a bounty,

up the bar ladder to the bay dive roof,

he drinks here.

Without duty, love is lined and proofed
in the last face he cannot see.

I was standing by the barstool with some niggas.
We was just 'bout to cross Nisqually tide.

The dirty water leaks below his port.
The dirty water crests above the port
and disrupts his visions in the waves.

And I ask if you would do my ass a favor,
take this message to her and the other side.

Dreams – in the fevered dockside – leave
as his last-call altar light dims.
His shore myth – in blackness – finally fails him
and the full tide taunts in nothingness.

If you see her, brother, tell her that you saw me,
and when you saw me, I was off my way.

Serpents above ground and in sea tales rhyme
down and up rickety levee docks.
Serpents in his rickety lit house mind
conflate shipman's dreams for facts.
They conflate her human wants for vices
in his loveless icy sky.
Then conflate no yarn, no harbor myths
to the end of a journey.

And if she asks where I am, tell her ...

Said the Ghetto Nerd to Narcissus at the Bar

You gazed in water, I stared in Hennessey.
What you ran to, I drank with blown-out eyes,
yet we both cannot identify life around us.
We, in stylized defeats of will,
turn clarity into slights of hand.
We, in the autumn of a misspent youth,
are wanderers self-created.

We argued who we died for – beauty or truth –
though the unseen in us magnifies the lie
that we gazed and named it cleanly,
that we fixed its fluid currents and movements
in allusions that became our cage.
In boasts that curdled into fits of pity,
we mistook vision for bluster.

Unable to leave, lord, how we hover.
Menageries of ruin and self-preserved youth
cue points on a cyclorama,
choking all metaphor into self-serving drama
that stayed still as we struggled to sell it.
Though we wanted to be seen
we could not make people see.
So fuck this bottle, I will leave.

Bully's Last Day on New Tacoma Ave

On the cold light day, he is banned from the block.
The rent-a-cop's shadow tags his peripheries
and tints the play inside his sherm-soaked
irises,
and touches the scenes that move as he moves
on his last day as a bully boy.
Windows break and re-break with every twitch
of his head.
Empty rights, beat-ins, abandoned mama's calls
footnote the 90-proof of his screams,
footnote the inaudible in the repetitive moans
in the sullen transfer of skies.
The wind straightens all fronts on the corner.
The boy-man holds his palms and swings
through the air
in an arc to his cheeks and ribs.
The transfer and bookings from bully to bum
are in rabbit holes paved by prodigals.

The Last Time I Saw Them, They Was Jump Roping

Beat points skip beside the street sweep.
Half-staff flags of yellow-brown and gold.

Your tongue ring is my northern star, love.

The sisters' soul clap. The sisters' spread sage.

The place and point where I will show all my hieroglyphs
that sign and mark my body.

By the ring shout the salt lamp
parallels with the chalk line
as it raises to the sky.

The rainbow over my variety of skies
that makes the wilderness worth it.

Colored dirt interacts with leaves and feet
then bounces off rock after rock.
Burnt soil flutters then melts in the street
then bounces off rock after rock
as the sisters continue to circle.

Take me, and I will walk with you.

Prayer groups kneel outside the gangstas.

Take me, and I will walk with you.

Prayer groups kneel outside the gangstas
as the sisters' transition to eighth claps.

Take me, and I will walk with you.

Prayer groups kneel outside the gangstas
as the sisters' transition to eighth claps
to find a beat key to the land.

I am a pilgrim, love, and a stranger to this.
Yet your varied lands and concentric circles
I will make my new threshing floors.
I will walk with you, changed,
in my adapting to your rebound.
Our leap, in tips and Harley black boots,
to better corners awaiting.

Why All the Wino's on 25th Street Turned Down God's Offer to Write a Book of the New Testament

He commands among a sea of tumbled dice.
He commands the men to stand up and witness
but they disintegrate (again) in the dust
and the mad dogs that close but still spin
as suit buttons gleam and arrange in the dark.
Corner hangouts, erased by the mysteries
of a blackout,
evaporate as if they were never there.
Who will write a book on my son?

And Willie went to his Zidovudine temples,
and Shermer Herman saluted to his son's Dead Sea.
and the defrocked OG spat bars to his rocks
and those he took in (and out) of that life.
Who will write a book on my son?

Holy words are adjectives of absence
and no one sees absence as sacrifice
from the trap house to the bar.
Dawn draws him a map to exit,
a time signature, but not a star.
Who will write a book on my son?

Treatise on Metaphor in the Wright Park Wading Pool When the Proud Boys Are in The Area

The metaphors of the wading pool double.
Agonies of the gravel floors still call the south
in juxtapositions of fleeing and relief.
Exuberances in generations of pools
washed clean by god turned blind
are only invisible to the nihilist.

The sundials of church hats
become walking shadows
children's runs to the water flash
are new then ancient.
Elders under the gray metal sprays
still dream of creeks without black bottoms.

No, dammit, no. I will not leave my pen.
I will not love the wound more than the mind.
I will not render my sense of the fantastic
into an altar for my scabs.
There is never a time to abandon the mind
under the northern Jackboot.
There is no time to abandon the mind.
I will write, dammit. I will write.

Landscape with Aunt Virginia, After She Smacked the Shit Out a Nigga for Macking at Women at a Funeral

After Antigone's first monologue

"If this what the nigga thinking
then we shouldn't have placed his ass there.
Not even asked the nigga to come.
He made his choice to wear them plaid pants, not wash his ass,
and slobber on that young girl.
He can be what the fuck he wants away from my babies.
But we got to bury this boy, and if he must
come here looking like his Zulu name
is 'Kehemet with the fake gold chain neck,'
then I will say this ass whipping is holy.
I shall lie down with the nigga in death
and make him as dear to me
as the porn and the MMA bill he puts in his baby's name.

It is the living,
Not the dead niggas, that make the longest demands, Bobby
Niggas die forever
but negroes do as they like
as the laws of God or love mean nothing to them,
in the scope of them getting some shit."

Bob's Bar-B-Q Pit Nightscape

The side fryer crackles
against the evening ice currents.
The wind's benign razors
straighten a city block
as a Sunday night line forms.

Hambone, hambone where you been?

Under uneven December spice clouds
the table is the unseen star.
Constellations of the side fryer
appear, then disappear
by the smoker's sodium sky.

Hambone, Hambone, where you been?

Beside the inside cook's alchemy
the wall painting mirrors.
Blues and yellows coordinate
with rack Sunday dresses.
Red and gray lapels
make priceless the Sunday bests.
Tones illuminate in watercolor witness
shape, movement, and rite.

The procession braces from another blast.
They rub their hands in the ice drafts
to get their daily meat and bread.
They put their palms toward each other
then in and out of their pockets
in a glimpse toward home in the concrete.

Hambone, Hambone, where you been?
All around the world and back again.
Hambone, Hambone, what you do?
Fixed you a sandwich. Eat some food.

Why Uncle Moe and Big Momma Danced by the Dirt Lamp When Their Song Came On

Together, they had no use for clear light
save a lamp to accent their stars;
save an outlier to reify shape
and make sense out of walls
and escape ports.
            I'll close my eyes

In the flicker, their bodies inhabit all space,
their touch, the dimension that stills all watches,
the circle unbroken in their invisible fractures
that make sense in the mazes between their arms.
                        to everyone but you

The day will have its facades of order.
Paint jobs and remakes run over themselves
to declare definition and ritual
to certify god into gilded-box pens
that scarlet up heaven and moral
to nows in beams and beaming grins
            modern propriety and order.
So they dance – in their smoke – in the dark,
the wino and the pool gangsta,
the mad poet and his cornbread anna,
dancing underground below the manors
waltzing in six-step by doors that revolve
but, in the black, never close.
                              and when I do, I'll see you standing there.

The Karaoke Bartender's Uber Note to God

Neither flood nor fire nor boils or pestilence
move us in the graveyard shifts
when you speak to midnight congregations.
Your gas-lit blue devils burn every stool
and singe every first and third Thursday.
Miracles unseen and second-borns gone
are the needles you stick in our eyes
when you tell us to believe.

Clothed and girded in the majesty
        of your parrot head
covering yourself with the light of your axe hat
stretching to all and everything you made
        before you made rum and scotch,
you end every sentence with "in paradise."
You call your congregation to remember in shots
of your light without redlined shadow,
of your dangling key star above shops,
storefronts, trains and underground death tunnels
(swept and swept over again while you boast).
Swept and provoked, we move when you point
your staff, then sing your karaoke song.

"Heeeeee butt the mud flap."
                                "It's 'Heat of The Moment,' pal."
"Heeeeeee butt the murmur."
                                "It's 'Heat of The Moment,' man."
"Wait ... Wait.... Heeeeeee-brew frank fart."
                                "Goddamnit."
"Wait. Wait ... Wait, give me another song."
                                "Get off the stage, man."
"Give me another song, bro!"
                                "Get the fuck off the stage."
"I am fucking God, goddamnit!! I made everything.
I made this song! I made the people in this song!

I made the instruments in this song!
And I made everything about the sweet kegger brokedown
that played this song!
This is the day that I made, bitches!
And If I want to sing another me damn song,
then me damnit, play me an Eddie Murphy song."
"An Eddie Murphy song?"

Oh god, who made the wide black sea
who kneaded the valleys and Sisyphean hills
who raised the river banks and bone-dimmed tides
raise yourself from the floor.
Raise yourself, your people are calling your son
to take this memory of refracted costs,
to take these reminders of sorrow and loss
and take your soiled-ass home.
"Too hot for the hot tub, ha!"
Oh god, get up. your clay is burning.
Your light that lit the steelhead
is drying its water.
Your moon that guided the raven
has led it now to slaughter

with the coyote and the turtle in repaved tracks.
"Hey hey"
"What, motherfucker"
"Can I borrow your phone?"
"You making hell look good, my man"
"Wait wait wait wait could you, could you"
"Could I do what? "
"Could you tell him I'm sorry for calling him a Black woke pussy
because he wouldn't thank me like the jocks?"

Oh god, you who made the grass and the dirt,
you alpha and omega with a smiley face shirt,
here's a cab, and here's 28 dollars.
Oh god, find yourself, go find yourself again.
Oh god, please go to the water.

Homie Didn't See the Wheel

I mess with Ezekiel again

1. Before his arrest, coming home from school

The brat packer's baggie is an invisible eclipse
a blind god of wilderness always two feet away
yet perilously, perilously close

through its white shadow, the bus stop unearths
from the gravel to the sky
distances from the corner to home
become unmeasurable
the slick polo sophomore is a cruel, hipster Solomon
and there is no one to plead in the gravel.

2. His arrest

"Not mine
That one
Spread em! Ground! Now!"

Head to your shoulder bone
In the gravel
Then your shoulder to your knee bone
Broke down
Then your knee to your thigh bone
Broke together
Then your knee to your thigh bone
Broke down

Round up
Lock down
Up state! Do time! Done time!

(This letter sets forth the full and complete plea offer to your client)
Your
(hereinafter referred to as "your client" or "defendant")
Boy
from the Special Counsel's Office (hereinafter also referred to as "the Government" or "this Office")
Is
(hereinafter also referred to as "the Government" or "this Office." This plea offer expires)

3. 27 Years after his arrest

Ezekiel, my bones are tired.
Judgments reign above the valley
yet why was my soul spared?
Judgments ring out arbitrarily
and the mosque is there then away
if at the whim of blue sticks.
Overflows in this vineyard
make phantasms of alleys
and hologram side corners
upon layers and layers of ruins.

The faces of creatures here aren't living.
Old commands turn to new rattlings.
Rims full of eyes both new and old
peer from hoods and hoods of squad cars.
New cities loom below cracked skies
as graves make the grounds tremor.
Exile and its markers blur truth and lies
and make myth the torturer of the beaten.
Ezekiel, Ezekiel, will my bones live.
Ezekiel, my bones are tired.

Ode to Keyboardists Who Play Niggas off When They Lie on the Dead in Funerals

How she plays on!
How she scrapes against the grace notes of false testimony
how she stopes the vestibule mixtape men
and upturns their selling tables
how she drags the dishonest in atonal harmonies.
If you pray right, heaven belong' to you.

Her pew hook is the shock
that makes false gods not touch,
the denotations that keep the infirmed
from getting "done up"
in perverse backroom streets
(those who don't have any more room
to receive).
If you sing right, heaven belong' to you.

Conquerors talk soft and sweetly of vengeance
conquerors talk on but not of us.
The sister blots the words
that have nothing to do with process
and redraws the axis of the ill buried.
If you love right heaven belong' to you.
If you love right.
If.

Brother's Arts Corner After the *Safe Streets* March, Searching for An Epiphany

It eludes us – a flicker there – then away
below it, ghetto birds cross
and cross each other

as beats and congas ram
in three-minute increments

below it, a storefront and the front of a bar
are a flood of people vexed by sirens
emcee's weave umpteen creation narratives
but the first ones with hair gone grey

below it, elders in faded African patterns
talk of blamelessness and youngbloods
talk over the dissonance that comes from leather patterns
syncopations that once held power.

Where are your drums, niggas? Where are they?
Where – of the black of night – is their power.
Why did you send them away?

Ode to The Sister Who Sells Hatbands at The Commerce Street Bus Station

First a king, then god,
then her mother in velvet,
then the motherland out of the fiber,
gold neon and twig.

Then the suns touch and eclipse each other.
Hot grey obscures fading flecks on Commerce
as she hustles her skies between stops.

The thick of fire smog dims the promise of sight
in a row of low-flying lamp suns.
Re-structured structures are mushed and obfuscated.
Posters and signs fade beside her glitter tints
and autumnal palates of neon.

Hers is a pattern out of no pattern:
a band and cover, both fixed and fluid,
woven from the untidy to become a stable agent
both structured and flexible in accompaniment,
both highlight and background of creation and form,
in the hazy dilapidation of the season.

Her hatbands are the air in declining air,
the background in the fluid,
the tidy in the abandoned, disparate mass
you can still touch and feel in the blank space.

Why Uncle Moe Played the Washboard When He Had Health Problems

Consumed by the silences
between his descriptive verbs
he seeks pattern if not sound
the repetition of motion,
sameness in step beyond
the notes and figures of sorrow songs
a self-same order in ivory soap and metal
beyond his affected scales.

It is motion, intimate in fiber, cleanliness,
King James and the James cook whip
subside from the worries of his mind.
In his hands and the birchwood,
in the wood chips and his elbow grease,
Cypress lays down classmates
weevils and wilding thug are cropped
in a time and tempo greater all his.

His washboard is the reify
of the failure of words,
the sum of his landscapes, pressing
of his synonyms,
the margins of the delta at the feet of his syllables,
a region toward home that gives a sense
in circumference
to routine-fated days.

The Procession After the Funeral Procession in Lakewood

The willows bend by us,
but in their own way.

Back and forth with the wind,
but cutting their own paces

between Gravelly Lake
and the fragments of the beach.

Black and white at night,
they reform our hair
in packs and scores of clusters.

Strategic intervals of blunts
in the forest
blurred anger, acidity, and time
in the lake she wouldn't have been at,

blurred rituals for the living
in drenched church clothed
in trespassed early June water.

They form their booths for her,
the willows in the dark lake.

They fix us up with the water bug
and the errant carnation.
They fly from the confines
of file and phylum
for the chance to give her a homegoing.

Not a Pop Trap Queen Funeral

Trees take after kinfolk, both distant and too close.
Holes in the 85-cracked wall replay
evidence of processions unseen,
the Bankhead service, families in Lincolns,
the going meal in the fish and hook spot,
the steampunk chariots in Chattahoochee Park
where we send her remnants to the river.
Phones playing the horn of a homegoing bounce
clear a path to her requested place,
funeral bois and gangsta girl vet
burn violets into sage into violets that fly
to where we lead her element and soil.
From this valley, our b-girl is leaving.
We shall miss her fly self and sweet smile.

Sons come back to iterations of storefronts.
Allegories of the saved ring from the red soils
as infirmed hoodlums kneel.
For drugs took all the street, Sista Sunshine,
who had brightened our block for a while?

On the ground we are the conquered, the unsaved,
the roadblocks and antagonists for victory and fable
the pestilence that spurred walls and mansions
that shadowed jails and fallout shelters.
We send her away (we, Faust's side kids),
offer our trap queen, more human than fable.
Lord, come sit by our sides if you love us,
if you hasten to bid us adieu.
Just remember our green river valleys.
and niggas who wanted to love you.

Notes on Alison Post's *Lighting the Way*

The clothesline is a reflection of slender threads.
The world must go on even if it's going.
The grass will grow when it isn't singed.

The weather scythes chaff that will make no breads.
Its winds blow nothing new even if it's still blowing.
The clothesline is a reflection of slender threads.

The thunderstorms make concentric rings
yet life has to have order even if it isn't spinning.
The grass will grow when it isn't singed.

The hills transform to fragile rosary beads.
The sky breaks but you can't be breaking.
The clothesline is a reflection of slender threads.

The globe is a cyclorama torn to the ends
yet one has to go on even if one is still living.
The grass will grow when it isn't singed.

Oh weary traveler, this station will end.
Oh weary traveler, you have to keep moving.
The clothesline is a reflection of slender threads.
The grass will grow when it isn't singed.

To the Juggalo Flexing at Me Downtown

Oh Juggalo, young Juggalo.
Sweet minstrel boy of gravel orchards.
Traveling pilgrim of binary corks
abandoned by tribes in the ice storm.

Somewhere to lay my head, somewhere to lay my head.

He wonders as he wanders the best he can,
Friends and the corner misunderstand
his candy clown symbols for warpaint.
Soft shoes in tandem with snazaroo masks
the callow 'buke and scorn him for.

Insanity, melting with the rain and sniffles,
raises thugs from the shadows;
the days and the hours between
the stomp and the troff
closing at the site of the harvest.

Somewhere to lay my head, somewhere to lay my head.

Wander as you wonder, sweet boy,
for the found tribes of hell are coming
and the river of sight
that befalls the lost jester
is blinding in ice and fire.

The Apocalypse Comes to the Detention Center

True believer, true believer, where you gonna run to?
The barren morning cages flash the final seal.
Soot makes the river that washes the swills
that took place by and over the water.

True believer, the sun is collapsing into dirt licks.
Sprinkles turn to hail over compounds and fences.
Steelheads and trails are gone in gateways
closed as the ground turns and turns.
The raven will ride the coyote to deliver
        their kinfolks
above quays tossed and burned.
True believer, true believer, where you gonna go?

True believer, this arc has no sign of the covenant.
Alms against a sea of troubles
open furnaces below children's tents.
Moons transform all homes, tidings, and kinfolk
in the blinding of this nothing sky.
The unseen will deliver what our id once denied
in the peril of what has been visible.
True believer, true believer, where you gonna go?

The ships have sailed in spite of their journey.
Blue ferrymen toil in new lit lakes.
Looks pass as vision for unseen eyes
and fences give boards but no shelter.

The sea will be filthy. The sea will be burning.
The beast will move in buildings above the dirt
in the captured hour come at last.
The beasts will inhabit the image of man
that circuits and troubles all sight.
The last shall be the first in that final seal night.
True believer, true believer, where you gonna run to?
True believer, true believer, where you gonna go?

Ode to Commencement Muralists

With a nod to "Gerontion" and the nigga that didn't get credit for writing Revelations

1.

At dawn, the painters stretch their hands.
No other city they know in the daybreak,
the day of judgment marks from clouds:
the easel's large-mass twin.
Voices that speak from golden lampstands
sing of bootleg meridians.

Pass us not, oh gentle savior.

They put trust in darkness remarked,
in wet slabs of brick, imagined mortar,
industry concrete reformed
                    to formlessness
by the miracle of Home Depot Krylon.
By the scrolls of seven blocks, their skies
are a blue too deep to go down,
are a blue too heavy for earth axis above them
and those suns burning red in their hues.

Pass us not, oh gentle savior.

And grass peeks in strokes and highlights.
And accented color coats vivify
the people in their skylines.
Their glad rags and spirits interplay
with chapels and mosques too slant
for instant decipherment
in the austerity of a city's Sunday sun.

Hear our humble cry.

Their clouds have a second life in layers ...
They move in their still shades
above their shadow towers.
Their windmills make a current
around tenements and states
of down-home deconstruction
cadences, in strokes are line breaks
decoded and recorded from the drum.

We are hood creatives,
do not pass us by.

In their new mosques and synagogues,
in their holy temples of paint
and italicized storefronts of recollection,
dead lambs take reincarnation
in symbols that linger
then annotate keys to disparate kingdoms.

Do not pass us by.

They sing in a pitch beyond perception.
High and low gather in the syndicates of
waters where their story and song are a raft.

Let us work, savior.
We will work, savior.
Do not pass us by.

2.

To the exile, home is a cacophony of the clear.
Neighborhood battles are zoned land da capos.
Tribes bicker and curse at the artists' feet
and sing of fires and marches to the sea.
Tribes call the artists to be swept away
over memes and social disgraces.
The emcee and influencer, Crip and vigilante cop,
fetishes in dream wars against each other:
imagined thug life, a bright cartoon sock hop

where they died and lived in nation fights,
where they died and lived in stolen hashtags
and gentrified revolution calls.
Rambos. Ankhs. Patriots. Bloods
Summer soldiers with bones long past and gone.

We all been gone to the river.

The artists alchemize conflict into their brushes.
By terrace ghosts, they work the concrete.
Foundations transfigured by matters of the needle
spring free from the sickness in their walls
that people below demand to purify,
spring free from the terror of arrested threads
of doxxers and Double Dutch drive-through Crips
long gone to blood and soil.

We all been gone to the river.

They create beyond the plaster of gutters.
They stride along paved tedious utters
in the tribalist's eternal November.
The lost tree of Lebanon is invisible among cedars.
Lambs stunt as lions as the seventh seal
is detectable yet in the air of all rage.
No horses come to save in the hill
where red is the symbol of sorrows.

We all been gone to the river.

Words on passages, pleas for respect,
are denied by bickering folks ears.
Words that ring through contrived Sunday corridors
turn to a thousand black horses –
turn to a thousand black gainly specters
deceived by whispering ambitious –
deceived by the vanities of boy-god charges
and the creators of a Frankensteinian eagle.
They fly for attention are distracted.
They fly above fedora strewn confusions.

They fly too late above what's not believed in
in the concrete sentimentality of memory.

Neither fear nor courage will save us,
our ghosts have turned to mirrors.
Unnatural heroism fathered by vices
rides above us and the moment is coming.

The artist is frantic, give their altar to the other
past edge lords and elder's flipped signals
past cities at war in toil and clutter

We all been gone to the river.

3.

On the right sides, crowds squat for a conclusion.
On the left, the ashy signify purpose.
The dumb and blind claim sanctity
in numbers around imagined devils.
In the November of the soul,
beauty is conflated with terror
in self-created portraits of the other.
Masks – in denial of shared sight, taste in touch –
are the prisons of souls in the dead quarter.

As we walk through the streets of the city.

Symbols are taken for wonders.
They only see the symbol,
they mistake daggers for crowns without royal order
in the eleventh hour. In a shiny, death-strewn corner,
the people await their Christ-brat child.

Yet the painters look up to their skies
they re-lace lost elders' rosary beads
in cornbread cubists blocks.
In that cornbread Avant-guard,
in that Young-G formalism

they raze stone images
then raise the binds of repression of the faded.

We will go sweeping through the city
where our homies and homegirls gone before.

Chariots of neon chrome fuse with low riders
in grey hills fused to lime valleys.

We will build by the banks of the river.
And be away from them no more.

In gold-chair staircase commencement alleys b-
boys and girls speak in tongues,
with round-a-way choirs resurrected by a boom box
that rumbles through pebble ground aisles
samples the soul clap

mix masters the holy ghost
bends unholy Piru thunder through the trombones
of shared marrows

goes step by step to higher mountains
and above the hill where the singular is written in fire.

One black morning, when hood life is over
we'll fly away
to a land where niggas never end
we'll fly away.
We'll fly away, hood niggas,
we'll fly away.
When we die and they burn us by and by
we'll fly away.

Gentle Savior,
B-boy Savior,
Homegirl Savior,
do not pass us by.
do not pass us by.

Value Village Love Poem

Old jackets don't fit, love, but did they ever?
Insignias and hats fade in the cycles
of discount trend racks.
Jerseys and spanks contract arbitrarily,
and scarfs hollow in the klieg lights
without the heads that gave them meaning.
Age and price may dictate our shape
but wherever you are is the boulevard.

Let me adorn you a crown of price-check rosaries.
Let my love be the alms that never signal
for without you, hoop earrings are metal,
extensions just threads away from their orbit,
away from their center and star.

Let them price to infinity
our posters and memories.
Let them splice the hood
to the meridians of invisibility.
In my arms, you are never gone.

My dear around-the-way girl,
dance with me by sale colors.
Time may erase all style to memory
but the intercom is playing our song.

1. Before He Broke Down in the Battle Rap

In islands of ice, in priest parking spaces
in Marriot yards of World Star altar calls
the boy-men hold blood devotion.

Discombobulated in verse, the old boy spits fire
that burns – for posterity – all his houses
that breaks himself out of all of his lineages
in an apex mirror of witness.
Loved ones and homies turn into witches
then circle and exit the parking lot
then swirl over ciphers and 808 traps
as the old boy denies his mother water
as the old boy turns his homes into rocks
on streets he runs but can never run to
as the old boy threads for the night needle's eye
of a record deal
till his opponent talked of hurting her.

2. After

Old boy, the roosters are getting louder.
Onlookers are gone to new gardens and gates
and opponents curb stomp you for weeping.
The productions close. The battles end.
Yet they still take your painted chain
as crows caw then fly from dying streetlights.
Tapes and vans take his pretense of artifice
but the jump is more real than reality.

In your dead land, hands are inverted eyes.
They redraw the faces of those you denied.
In Safeway parking lot faces
old boy, old boy, in the redlined wilderness
you have no hiding places.

Blues for Mr. James, The Last Guardian

When he cannot tell you, the answer becomes all of them.
The gothic northern line, spackled greyhound station,
museums castle-like, and then Art Deco,
restaurants and trap houses that switch perilous places
every time you turn to look.

Above the rippled binoculars of his flask,
he sweeps then is stopped by his city.
Through his fuzzed, decanted eyes,
black collars cross their shadow boys at the PAL.
Sisters of the jump rope cannot leap for exemption
in the shadow of patrol stops for children.
Swiveled head and new street survivors,
ones he ferried to safety in their same land,
walk past the linked riverbanks of their blues.

Soldiers are invisible yet possess all that moves him,
his gulfs between the world and store owners.
His blue lines restrict but can never be leaned on
as he struggles to define stations and homes.

"Oh, ferryman, you can weep. You can moan.
Love is a tenuous mirror house of the individual.
The air and sun of the deliverer's day
has a bottom that knows no floors.
The ships that left you are not tossed and driven
Oh, ferryman, you can weep."

About the Author

Robert Lashley is a writer and activist. He is a 2016 Jack Straw Fellow, Artist Trust Fellow, and a nominee for a Stranger Genius Award. He has had work published in The *Seattle Review of Books, NAILED, Poetry Northwest, McSweeney's*, and *The Cascadia Review.* His poetry was also featured in such anthologies as *Many Trails to The Summitt, Foot Bridge Above the Falls, Get Lit, Make It True*, and *It Was Written.* His previous books include *The Homeboy Songs* (Small Doggies Press, 2014), and *Up South* (Small Doggies Press, 2017). In 2019, *The Homeboy Songs* was named by *Entropy Magazine* as one of the 25 most essential books to come out of the Seattle area.

More Poetry by Robert Lashley

Up South (2017)

The Homeboy Songs (2014)